The Kingdom Man Rising

Table of contents

Introduction

Focus of Week One……..
    *Truth in Identity
      *Calling.

Focus of Week Two…….
    *Becoming "The Kingdom Man"
    * Character
      * Integrity.

Focus of Week Three.....

* Relationships

* Brotherhood

* Connection

* Unity

* Strength Through Godly Relationships

Focus of Week Four....

* Purpose

* Legacy

* Faith in Action

* "The Kingdom Man's" Walk

* Shaping The World Around You

* One in Christ

Introduction

- Rise Up
- Lead
- Conquer
- Overcome
- Receive Your Crown

You were never meant to live an ordinary life.

Inside every man is the heartbeat of a warrior — called to rise in faith, walk in purpose, and burn with the fire of the Holy Spirit.

In The Kingdom Man Rising: 30 Days of Faith, Fire, and Purpose, Thomas Lee Hurd leads you through a powerful journey of transformation from……faith to faith…..strength to strength….golry to glory building "The Kingdom Man"

Each day combines Scripture, reflection, prayer, and action. These steps will strengthen your spirit man, build your confidence in Christ, renew your mind, and awaken your divine calling in the manifestation of "The Kingdom Man".

Through this 30-day experience, you will:

- Rediscover your true identity as a man created in God's image.

- Learn to lead your family, relationships, and purpose with confidence and humility.

- Build spiritual discipline, courage, and endurance through the storms of life.

- Catch fresh fire from the Holy Spirit and live with Kingdom authority.

This is not just devotional — it's a movement.

A call to rise as the man God destined you to be: fearless, faithful, and filled with fire.

It's time to stand up.

It's time to lead.

It's time to become The Kingdom Man Rising.

A man who Kneels before god can stand before any man

.....Week One.....

*Identity   *Calling

Day 1: Created in His Image

Scripture:

"So God created man in His own image; in the image of God He created him; male and female He created them." — Genesis 1:27

Reflection

Before you ever took your first steps, swung a hammer, led a meeting, or prayed your first prayer, God stamped His image on you. Before the foundation of the world he knew you and the plans he made for your life.

You are not a mistake. You are not a product of your past. You are the intentional design of a Creator who shaped you with purpose, strength, soul, and spirit. You are climbing the mountain of the lord with intention and purpose.

When life beats you down or when others misjudge your worth, remember this: your identity doesn't begin with what you've done — it begins with who He is and who he called you to be —

The God who created mountains, galaxies, and oceans looked at all of it and said, "Let Us make man in Our image." That means every part of you — your mind, your will, your ability to love and create — is a reflection of the divine.

God said it is very good!

(Genesis 1:31)

But being made in His image isn't about power; it's about presence. God didn't make men to dominate but to dwell in him and represent Him — His character, His compassion, His courage. The world doesn't need perfect men; it needs men who remember whose image they bear and carry the light.

The greater Kingdom will dominate and overtake the lesser.

Each morning you wake up, you have the chance to walk in that truth — to live as a son of God, not a slave to sin. You are not defined by failure; you are defined by your Father in heaven. Pick up the daily burdens and follow..Him   *(Matthew 16:24)*

Call to Action

Stand in front of a mirror today and speak this aloud:

"I am made in the image of God. I am chosen, called, and created for His glory, I AM a Kingdom Man Rising"

Declare

I can do all things through Christ who strengthens me!

Now take five minutes to thank God for one unique quality and abilities. **He placed inside of you** — something that reflects Him (creativity, patience, strength, compassion, etc.).

Reflect, use the power of your words to begin to thank God for his goodness, how he created you and thank him for the spirit of grace. Begin to recognize the things you can be grateful for (ability to walk, talk, run, breath, etc) enter the gate through praise and thanksgiving.   *(John 6:11)*

Prayer,

Father in heaven, thank You for creating me in Your image and likeness.

Remind me that my worth isn't in what I do or have done in the past but my value is in who You are and who you have made me to be. My worth is the price that Jesus The Christ paid on the cross at calvary. Father, Strengthen me, shape my heart to reflect Your goodness, grace and mercy today. Out of my new heart will flow rivers of living water. *(Ezekiel 36:26)*

In Jesus' mighty name, amen.

Day 2: A Man After God's Heart

Scripture:

"And when He had removed him, He raised up David to be their king, of whom He testified and said, 'I have found David the son of Jesse, a man after My own heart, who will do all My will.'" — Acts 13:22

Reflection

The Kingdom Man is a man in pursuit, a man who is intentional and carries purpose. David was not a perfect man. He failed, stumbled, and made choices that wounded others and grieved God. Yet God still called him…..

"a man after My own heart."

That's the mystery of grace and the beauty of divine relationship — God isn't looking for flawless men; He's looking for faithful men. Men whose hearts beat in rhythm with His. Men who, even when they fall, fall toward Him instead of away from Him.

David's greatness wasn't found in his strength, but in his surrender. He knew where his help came from. When he was confronted with sin, he repented. When he faced giants, he trusted. When he was alone in caves, he worshiped.

Being a man after God's heart means choosing intimacy over image — it's about seeking God in private before leading in public. It's letting your heart stay soft before Him, even when the world hardens you.

Every Kingdom Man Rising will face seasons where their faith is tested and it feels easier to compromise, to drift, to hide, or to build walls of offence. But the heart that pursues God — even imperfectly — becomes the kind of heart God can use mightily.

He's not looking for your perfection. He's looking for your pursuit.

Choose progress over perfection.

Action Step

Find a quiet place today. Ask the Holy Spirit to reveal if there's any part of your heart you've withheld from God — maybe pride, bitterness, fear, rejection, shame, trauma, abuse.

Ask the Holy Spirit to reveal the walls and cast light upon your understanding. *(proverbs 3:5)*

Write it down, surrender it, and pray for a heart that beats after His. Remember God is near the broken hearted.

(Psalm 34:18)

Prayer,

Lord, make me a Kingdom Man after Your own heart.

Teach me to love what You love and to turn quickly when I fall.

Lead me by your Spirit into my inheritance of The Kingdom.

Lead me in paths of peace that transcends beyond my natural understanding. Lead me paths righteousness and take me to a place to rest in you.

Deliver me from evil and let my life reflect Your mercy and my heart stay open to Your will. In Jesus' name, amen.

(Psalm 23:3)

Notes_____

Day 3: Walking in Purpose

Scripture:

"For we are His workmanship, created in Christ Jesus for good works, which God prepared beforehand that we should walk in them." — Ephesians 2:10

Reflection

You were not created to wander aimlessly through life.

You were crafted — intentionally designed — for a divine purpose that God prepared long before you took your first breath.

Every Kingdom Man who walks with Jesus must come to this truth: purpose is not something you invent; it's something you discover and receive from Him. The closer you walk with Christ, the clearer your calling becomes and the more He adds to your life.   *(Matthew 6:33)*

We live in a world obsessed with performance and status. But kingdom purpose flows from relationship, not recognition.

It's not about titles or applause; it's about obedience. The carpenter from Nazareth didn't chase fame — He simply walked in what the Father had called Him to do. And that walk changed eternity.

(Phillipians 2:7)

Your steps matter. Every act of faithfulness, every word of encouragement, every quiet decision to live with integrity — it all builds the testimony of a man who knows who he belongs to.

The Kingdom Man doesn't change his ways according to who may be watching or if no person or people are is sight because he realizes that everything is done before an audience of ONE   *(Matthew 9:13) (Proverbs 3:5-6)*

Sometimes purpose feels hidden. You may not see the fruit right away. But remember: a seed planted in obedience will always grow in due season. God brings the increase. The goal isn't to rush ahead of God, but to walk with Him — one step at a time one word at a time. The Kingdom Man does not live on bread alone but every word that proceeds from the mouth of God.

(Matthew 4:4)

When you *rise up* and walk in your divine purpose, you will automatically stop chasing everything else. You find peace and fulfillment in the path He's already prepared for you. The mind is a great servant but a terrible master. This is why we must put on the mind of Christ.   *(Phillipians 2:5-11)*

Notes_____

Action Step

Take a few minutes today to pray and journal:

What "good works" might God have already placed in front of you?

What has God directed you to do that you have not done or became disobedient and then compromised?

It could be mentoring someone younger, serving your church, or being a light at work.

It could be a prophetic dream that God gave and you answered or rejected.

This can do with starting a business or giving up something that you think you need.

It could be anything that God has spoken that you are doing or have already done.

Reflect on this area of your walk and write them down.

Write one step you can take today to walk in that purpose — and do it.

If you like sports, think of this…can your favorite team win the game if they only play defence? No. It's not possible. The best they can hope for is an even score.

This is survival at best…You're not called to survive, you're called to live in a life of abundance and overflow. *(John 10:10)*

The Kingdom Man is proactive and gets things done for his Kingdom but he must understand his purpose and where he gets his direction, power and wisdom from.

The King Of Kings

We win by walking in obedience and overcoming in....Victory

(Revelation 3:21)

(revelation 21:7)

Notes_____

Prayer

Lord, thank You for designing me with divine purpose.

Help me walk in step with Your will and Kingdom purpose add supernatural power in my walk from this day forward, not striving to make my own way or out of my own strength but by your divine dunamis power.

Order my steps today, encounter me in dreams,

visions and may I receive divine visitation from

heaven. Encourage me by your prophetic word that

builds, edifies and encourages my Kingdom walk.

Let my life bring glory to You. In Jesus' name, amen.

(John 5:19-20)

Day 4: God's Strength, Not My Own

Scripture:

"But he said to me, 'My grace is sufficient for you, for my power is made perfect in weakness.' Therefore I will boast all the more gladly about my weaknesses, so that Christ's power may rest on me." — 2 Corinthians 12:9

Reflection

Every man wants to be strong — to stand tall, carry weight, and protect those he loves. But the kind of strength God calls us to doesn't start in muscle or mind; it begins in dependence.

The Apostle Paul learned this the hard way. He faced thorns, trials, and pressures that drove him to his knees. But instead of removing his pain, God revealed His purpose: "My power is made perfect in weakness."

That's the paradox of the Kingdom — where the world says "be self made," Jesus says "be Spirit-led." Where the world says "never let them see you struggle," God says "My strength shows through your surrender."

It's not weakness to admit you need help — it's wisdom. A real man of faith understands that strength apart from God leads to pride, but strength in God leads to power, peace, and perseverance.

When you stop pretending to be invincible, you make room for God's power to flow. You become the kind of Kingdom Man who can lift others up —
not because you're unbreakable, but because you've learned who holds you together.

Your strength doesn't come from your willpower — it comes from the will of God and his word spoken over your life. His presence and the Spirit Of Grace. Every burden you place in His hands is a battle you no longer have to fight alone after all its his plan.

The Kingdom can not be shaken *(Hebrews 12:28)*

Action Step

Think of one area of your life where you've been relying on your own strength — maybe a habit, a relationship, or a hidden fear.

Pray over it today and consciously hand it over to God. Ask Him to be your strength where you are weak.

You were not born with a spirit of fear but of power, love and a sound mind. *(2 Timothy 1:7)*

Ask and it shall be given..seek and you will find.. (Matthew 7:7)

Ask the Holy Spirit If you have been acting in fear and in a double minded way. Ask the Holy Spirit to minister to those areas to bring light, comfort and direction in the way of power, love and a sound mind.

Write down what that surrender to his will looks like in action this week.

Notes_____

Prayer

Lord, I admit that I can't do it all on my own.

Be my strength and the rock and solid foundation in my life. Visit the places where I am weak and helpless.

Your power is perfect in my weakness.

Release your power on my life from this day forward that I will never be the same.

Change me into your image from strength to strength and glory to glory.

Let Your power rest on me and teach me to lean on Your grace

daily. In Jesus' name, amen.

Notes_____

Day 5: Living Unashamed

Scripture:

"For I am not ashamed of the gospel, because it is the power of God that brings salvation to everyone who believes." — Romans 1:16

Reflection

There's something bold and freeing about a man who's unashamed of Jesus.

He doesn't hide his faith when the world mocks it. He doesn't shrink back when others question it. He walks in truth with quiet confidence — not to prove himself, but to honor the One who saved him.

Paul's words ring like a battle cry for every believer: "I am not ashamed of the gospel." Why? Because he knew what that gospel had done for him. The same man who once persecuted the church became one of its greatest voices. Grace had changed him, and he refused to be silent about it.

The world often tells men to keep faith private — to separate belief from real life. But The Kingdom Man knows his faith is his life. It shapes how he loves, leads, and serves.

Being unashamed doesn't mean being loud; it means being authentic. It's when your life quietly preaches before your lips ever do.

When you stand firm in your faith, people notice. And sometimes, the very ones who mocked you will come back asking where your peace comes from. That's the power of living unashamed — it points others to the Source of your strength.

Never apologize for your devotion to Jesus.

The cross may offend some, but it's also the only thing that truly saves. *(Matthew 10:33)*

Action Step

Be intentional about showing your faith today.

That could mean praying over your meal in public, encouraging a coworker, or sharing what God's done in your life with a friend.
Ask God to give you courage to live your faith openly, not arrogantly — but confidently, as His representative.
Ask him to show you who he wants you to visit or put in your path and pray for or minister to.
The Kingdom Man is intentional when asking for direction from the Father.

Prayer

Lord, give me boldness to live unashamed of You.

Let my actions and words reflect Your love and Spirit Of Truth. Help me produce fruit that remains and will not perish. Help me direct others to your Kingdom and their divine purpose and calling in the Spirit Of Prophecy. Give me divine revelation not only for my own life but for the lives of others around me. May my life point others to the saving grace of salvation in Christ. Let your name be lifted high above all others. I stand on the Rock , amen.

Day 6: Standing Firm in Faith

Scripture:

"Be on your guard; stand firm in the faith; be courageous; be strong. Do everything in love." — 1 Corinthians 16:13–14

Reflection

Every man of God will face moments when faith is tested — when the winds of doubt blow hard and the ground beneath you shakes.

In those moments, God's call is not to panic or retreat, but to stand firm.

Faith isn't proven in comfort; it's proven in conflict. Anyone can believe when life is smooth, but true faith stands when the storm hits. It's the faith that refuses to bow to fear, that clings to God's promises even when nothing makes sense.

Paul's words are both a warning and a charge: "Be on your guard. Stand firm. Be courageous. Be strong." But notice how he ends it: "Do everything in love."

That's the balance of The Kingdom Man — strength anchored in love. Bold but humble. Firm but compassionate.
Standing firm doesn't mean being stubborn. It means being rooted — planted deep enough in Christ that no trial can uproot you. The enemy doesn't fear a man who goes to church; he fears

a man whose faith stands unshaken when pressure comes.

When you know who your God is, you don't need to fight for victory — you fight from victory. The cross has already settled the outcome. All that's left is for you to stand your ground, clothed in truth, peace, and righteousness. *(John 16:33)*

Action Step

Think of one area in your life where your faith has been shaken — maybe in finances, relationships, or purpose.

Today, write down a Scripture that speaks directly to that situation. Declare it out loud when doubt or fear arises.

Your faith grows stronger each time you choose to stand instead of run. *(James 1:2)*

Prayer

Father, anchor my heart in You when the storms come and help me to remember the call and purpose according to your will. I choose to count it as joy when my faith is tested because you are bringing thee increase and victory upon my Kingdom walk. Help me to stand firm in faith and act in love no matter what I face. As it is written, let my faith please you and grow from a mustard seed into the Kingdom tree that supports life.

May you be pleased by my faith and obedience.

Let my courage rise from trust in Your promises, not in my own strength.

In Jesus' name, amen.

Day 7: Called to Lead in Love

Scripture:

"The greatest among you will be your servant." — Matthew 23:11

Reflection

Leadership in the Kingdom doesn't look like leadership in the world. The world measures greatness by how many people serve you. Jesus measures greatness by how many people you serve.

Every man is called to lead in some capacity — in his home, his work, his church, or his community. But real leadership isn't about control or status; it's about love in action.

Jesus, the ultimate King, took off His robe, wrapped a towel around His waist, and washed His disciples' feet. That's the image of godly leadership — strength under submission, authority expressed through humility.

To lead in love means to guide others not by force, but by example. It's showing patience when others test you, grace when others fail you, and consistency when others depend on you. The most powerful men in the Kingdom are those who know how to kneel. *(Matthew 20:26)*

When a man leads in love, he becomes a reflection of Christ's character — firm but gentle, bold but compassionate. His influence doesn't come from demanding respect; it flows from earning trust through faithfulness.

Ask yourself today: Am I leading with love or just leading with pride? The difference determines whether your leadership builds people up or breaks them down.

God has called you to be a leader — not to be served, but to serve with love.

Here are 6 Kingdom Man Leadership Keys

1. It's not about control but service
2. It's not about obtaining power over others but empowering others.
3. It's not about manipulation but about inspiration.
4. It's not about people but purpose. God aligns purpose.
5. It's not about being led by money, feelings, needs or emotions..Kingdom Leaders are led by the Spirit.
6. It's not about trying to get them to love you, it's about becoming love and your life is the leader by example.

Love never fails (1 Corinthians 13:8)

Action Step
Look for one person today you can serve — not because you have to, but because you get to.

It could be helping a coworker, encouraging your spouse, or mentoring a younger man in faith.

Ask God to open your eyes to opportunities to lead by loving.

Prayer

Father, thank You for calling me to lead with love.

Teach me to lead like The Kingdom Man — with humility, patience, and strength. Let my leadership bring **Miracles, Deliverance, Healing, Hope, Breakthrough, Destiny, Revelation, Calling, Salvation and Honor** to Your Kingdom. In Jesus' name, amen.

Week 2

The Kingdom Man. Character and Integrity.

Day 8: The Power of Humility

Scripture:

"Humble yourselves, therefore, under God's mighty hand, that he may lift you up in due time." — 1 Peter 5:6

Reflection

True strength begins with humility.

The world celebrates pride — being self-made, self-assured, and self-promoting — but the Kingdom of God moves in the opposite direction. The way up is down. The path to greatness begins on your knees.

Humility doesn't mean weakness; it means wisdom. It's recognizing who you are in Christ and who the Father is — and understanding that everything good in you flows from His hand. The humble man doesn't have to prove himself; he rests in who the Father says he is.

David didn't become king because he demanded it. He was anointed in obscurity while tending sheep. Joseph didn't reach the palace because of ambition; he got there through years of humility in prisons and pits. Jesus Himself — the Son of God — "humbled Himself and became obedient to death, even death on a cross."

When you walk in humility, you create space for God to move. Pride closes the door to His blessing, but humility opens it wide. *(James 4:6)*

And here's the truth — the man who kneels before God can stand tall before anyone.

God doesn't forget the humble. In His timing, He will lift you up, promote you, and trust you with more. Until then, stay low. Stay teachable. Stay grateful. *(Matthew 23:12)*

Action Step

Every Kingdom has laws, authority, structure and purpose. Jesus said there is different authority given to the humble and the meek will inherit the earth.

Your breakthrough is hidden in humility for greater authority in The Kingdom.

Ask the Holy Spirit to show you one or more areas where pride has quietly taken root — maybe in your attitude, words, or relationships.

Confess it and replace it with gratitude.

Then look for one way to serve someone today without needing recognition or credit. *(Matthew 6:3)*

Prayer

Lord, teach me the strength and value of humility.

Help me to lay down pride and walk with a servant's heart.

Bring Power and Authority in my Kingdom life and ministry.

Lift me in Your timing, and let my life reflect Your Image, not my ego. In Jesus' name, amen.

Day 9: Courage Under Fire

Scripture:

"Have I not commanded you? Be strong and courageous. Do not be afraid; do not be discouraged, for the Lord your God will be with you wherever you go." — Joshua 1:9

Reflection

Courage isn't the absence of fear — it's faith that refuses to bow to it.

Joshua knew what it felt like to face impossible odds. Standing before the Promised Land, he saw giants, fortified cities, and uncertainty stretching out before him. Yet God's command wasn't complicated: "Be strong and courageous."

David stood strong and courageous to defeat Goliath..Courage under fire.

Those words weren't a suggestion; they were a divine order — rooted in the promise of God's presence. "For the Lord your God will be with you wherever you go." That's the source of real courage. *(Romans 8:31)*

As men, we often face fires that test our resolve — financial pressure, family conflict, moral temptation, spiritual opposition. Courage under fire doesn't mean pretending it's easy; it means pressing forward even when your knees shake.

Kingdom courage is born when a man trusts that God is bigger than what he's facing.

It's the father who keeps praying for a wayward son.

It's the husband who chooses faithfulness when the world

tempts him to quit.

> It's the believer who stands for truth when everyone else stays silent.

The fire you face today might feel intense, but it's also refining you. God uses fire to strengthen your faith, not destroy it. The same flames that threaten to consume you can become the very ones that forge your testimony.

So, when the heat rises, don't retreat — remember who walks through the fire with you. *(Daniel 3:25)*

Action Step

Identify one area where fear has been holding you back — maybe a decision, a conversation, or a step of faith.

Write it down and bring it before God in prayer.

Then take one small, bold action today that aligns with faith instead of fear.

Prayer

Father, give me courage and boldness when fear tries to

silence me. Help me to remember that You are with me

in every battle and you will never leave or forsake me.

I receive a fresh baptism of your fire.

Let my faith grow stronger in the fire, and may my courage bring glory to Your name.

In Jesus' name, amen.

Day 10: Integrity in the Dark

Scripture:

"The integrity of the upright guides them, but the unfaithful are destroyed by their duplicity." — Proverbs 11:3 (NIV)
Reflection

Integrity is who you are when no one's watching.

It's not built in the spotlight; it's forged in **The Secret Place** — in quiet choices, unseen moments, and private thoughts.

Every man faces a decision between what's easy and what's right. The world says, "Do what works." God says, "Do what's true."

Integrity is the difference between those two paths.

Joseph understood this. Alone in Egypt, far from family, he could have compromised when temptation came knocking. No one would've known — but God would have. And Joseph's refusal to sin didn't just protect his purity; it preserved his destiny.

That's what integrity does — it anchors your future in faithfulness. When you live with integrity, your word carries weight, your actions align with your beliefs, and your life points people to the character of Christ.

But integrity will always be tested in the dark. When no one's around, when shortcuts look tempting, or when the crowd goes the other way — that's where character is proven.

A man of integrity may not always be noticed, but he will always be trusted.

You don't need to be perfect — just consistent. God honors the man who chooses righteousness when no one else will.

This is how we worship in Truth….(John 4:24)

Action Step

Reflect today on one private area of your life where you're tempted to compromise — maybe how you handle money, conversations, or what you entertain your mind with.

Ask God for strength to live in integrity even when no one sees. Choose truth over convenience or compromise.

(Matthew 5:27)

Prayer

Lord, keep my heart pure and my motives clean.

Help me to walk with integrity in every hidden place of my life.

Help me to cast down vain imagination and thoughts of this world.

Give me Kingdom thoughts and wisdom.

May my private choices bring honor to You and strength to my witness.

In Jesus' name, amen.

Day 11: Overcoming Temptation

Scripture:

"No temptation has overtaken you except what is common to mankind. And God is faithful; He will not let you be tempted beyond what you can bear. But when you are tempted, He will also provide a way out so that you can endure it." — 1 Corinthians 10:13

Reflection

Every man faces temptation — it's part of the human battle. But the good news is this: temptation is not sin. It's the moment before the choice — and in that moment, God always provides a way out.

Even Jesus was tempted in the wilderness. The enemy came at Him with lies and half-truths, trying to twist His purpose. But Jesus didn't fight with emotion; He fought with the Word from a place of Love and Zeal for the Father. "It is written." That's how victory is won — not through willpower, but through truth and dependence on God's strength and purpose of his Kingdom.

Temptation often comes when we're tired, lonely, or feeling unseen. The enemy looks for weakness, but God uses those same moments to grow discipline and discernment in us. Each time you resist, your
spiritual muscles grow stronger. Each time you choose obedience, your heart becomes more aligned with His.

You don't have to face it alone. The Holy Spirit lives in you — and He's stronger than any temptation that comes against you. You may have fallen before, but today is a new day. Grace is not permission to sin — it's power to overcome it.

Remember: you're not fighting for purity; you're fighting from victory. The cross already broke sin's grip. Your part is to walk in that freedom, one choice at a time.

(James 4:7)

Action Step

Think of one recurring temptation in your life.

Identify the moments or emotions that usually trigger it.

Then, find a Scripture that speaks truth against that lie — memorize it and speak it whenever temptation arises.

If needed, share your struggle with a trusted brother in Christ for accountability. *(James 5:16)*

Prayer

Father, thank You for giving me power over

temptation and the Spirit of Truth. Remind me that I

am not a slave to sin, but free in Christ.

Help me to see the way of escape You provide and give me the strength to take it.

In Jesus' name, amen.

Day 12: Faithful in the Little

Scripture:
"Whoever can be trusted with very little can also be trusted with much, and whoever is dishonest with very little will also be dishonest with much." — Luke 16:10

Reflection

Every great man of God started small.

Before David ruled a kingdom, he tended sheep. Before Joseph managed a nation, he managed a prison. Before Jesus began His ministry, He quietly worked as a carpenter.

Faithfulness in the little things prepares you for the larger ones. God uses small, hidden seasons to test and strengthen your heart. It's in the unseen places — the daily disciplines, the quiet acts of obedience — that character is built.

The world tells men to chase big platforms and quick results. But the Kingdom operates differently. Promotion doesn't come from hustling — it comes from honoring. When you're faithful with what's in your hands now, God can trust you with what's in His.

Sometimes faithfulness feels unnoticed. You serve, give, and show up, and it seems like no one sees. But Heaven is always watching. Every moment of obedience counts. Every unseen act of integrity is an investment in your destiny.

God never wastes faithfulness. What looks small today may be the seed of something extraordinary tomorrow.

So stay steady. Keep showing up. Keep being faithful — not for recognition, but because it honors the One who called you.

Gifts are free and come without repentance but character must be cultivated.

Action Step

Look around your life today — your work, your home, your relationships.

Identify one "small" area where God is asking you to be more consistent or intentional.

It could be prayer in The Secret Place, time with your family, or diligence in your job quality. Commit to doing it faithfully for the next seven days.

Prayer

Lord, thank You for trusting me with what I have today.

Teach me to be faithful in the small things and patient in the process.

I know You're preparing me for greater things as I honor You in the little ones.

In Jesus' name, amen.

Day 13: Godly Wisdom

Scripture:

"If any of you lacks wisdom, you should ask God, who gives generously to all without finding fault, and it will be given to you." — James 1:5

Reflection

Wisdom is one of the greatest treasures a man can possess — and one of the rarest.

Knowledge can be learned, but wisdom must be received. It's not about how much you know, but how well you listen to Heaven.

Solomon could have asked God for riches, fame, or power, but instead he asked for wisdom — the ability to discern right from wrong and lead with understanding. That prayer pleased God so much that He gave Solomon not only wisdom, but also everything he didn't ask for.

That's the power of godly wisdom — it attracts God's favor because it puts His heart first.

Wisdom doesn't always shout; it often whispers. It's found in stillness, in prayer, and in the quiet counsel of the Holy Spirit. It helps you pause before reacting, think before speaking, and choose faith over impulse.

The enemy loves to rush men into decisions. God invites you to wait and discern. The wise man doesn't move faster — he moves smarter, led by the peace of God instead of the pressure of people.

When you walk in godly wisdom, you'll notice something changes

— less chaos, fewer regrets, and more fruit. Wisdom turns mistakes into lessons and challenges into growth. It's not perfection; it's perspective.

Wisdom without measure (James 1:5)

Action Step

Take one decision you're currently facing — big or small — and bring it before God in prayer.

Instead of asking Him to give you what you want, ask Him to show you what's right.

Then, take time to listen. Sometimes wisdom comes not in a shout, but in a still, small voice.

The Kingdom Man understands that a greater than Solomon is here and has made himself available in all wisdom to the believer. (Matthew 12:42)

Prayer
Father, I stand in faith for Your wisdom today. You promise to give without measure. **I received it!**

Teach me to think with the mind of Christ and to walk in discernment and knowledge of your Kingdom.

Let every choice I make reflect Your truth and bring direction and peace to my path.

In Jesus' name, amen.

Day 14: The Warrior Spirit

Scripture:

"Blessed be the Lord, my rock, who trains my hands for war, and my fingers for battle." — Psalm 144:1

Reflection

Every man who walks with God carries within him the heart of a warrior.

Not a fighter for fame or ego, but a soldier for the Kingdom — called to stand, defend, and conquer in the Spirit.

David wrote those words as both a shepherd and a soldier. He understood that his real battles weren't just fought with swords but in the unseen realm — battles for purity, faith, and obedience. God Himself was his trainer, shaping his hands for physical battle and his heart for spiritual warfare. *(1John 2:27)*

The world may not understand it, but The Kingdom Man is not passive — he is purposeful. He battles and fights in his prayers, stands in truth, and protects his home, his mind, and his calling from the enemy's plans and schemes.

The true warrior doesn't fight people — he fights principalities. His power doesn't come from anger, but from authority in Christ and his Kingdom. *(1Corinthians 4:20)*

When you embrace your warrior spirit, you stop retreating from challenges and start advancing in faith. The fight isn't easy — it never was meant to be — but you are not alone in it. The

Commander of Heaven's armies stands beside you.

Put on your armor. Stand your ground.

Your family, your faith, and your future are worth fighting for.

Action Step

Spend a few minutes in prayer today using your voice, declaring victory over the areas of your life where the enemy has tried to gain ground — your mind, your marriage, your purpose, or your peace.

Write down three "battles" you are currently facing and speak God's promises over each one.

Prayer

Lord, train my hands for battle and my heart for peace. Empower me to fight not in anger, but in authority through Your Holy Spirit. Let me be strong, mighty, steady, and unshaken as I stand in Your Kingdom, Power and Glory. In Jesus' name, amen.

Notes_____

Week 3: Relationships

— a week centered on connection, unity, and strength through godly relationships.

Day 15: Iron Sharpens Iron

Scripture:
"As iron sharpens iron, so one man sharpens another." — Proverbs 27:17

Reflection

Every man needs other men.

God said it's not good for man to be alone.

No matter how strong, spiritual, or independent you think you are, God never designed you to walk alone.

When iron sharpens iron, sparks fly — but that's what makes both pieces stronger. Brotherhood in Christ isn't always comfortable; it's honest, challenging, and refining. Real men of God don't flatter you — they sharpen you. They speak truth when you're slipping, pray when you're weak, and stand with you when life hits hard.

The enemy loves isolation. He knows that a lone man is an easy target. That's why God builds strength in community — in friendships that are rooted in faith, accountability, and prayer.

Look at Jesus: even He didn't walk alone. He surrounded Himself with brothers — men He taught, loved, and trusted.

The disciples didn't always get it right, but they grew stronger together. That's the power of brotherhood — imperfect men chasing a perfect Savior, side by side.

A true brother doesn't compete with you; he completes what's lacking in you. He helps you see blind spots, celebrate victories, and stay anchored in truth.

And when you sharpen each other in love, you both become more effective for God's Kingdom.

Jesus couldn't fulfil his call apart from Judas some will betray you.

Action Step

Think about the men in your circle.
Who sharpens you spiritually? Who challenges you to grow?

Reach out to one brother today — send an encouraging message, pray together, or simply check in.

If you don't have men like that in your life, ask God to bring them — and be willing to be that man for someone else.

Prayer

Lord, thank You for the brothers You've placed in my life. Help me to build relationships that sharpen and strengthen faith.

Make me a man who lifts others up, speaks truth in love, and stands firm in unity.

In Jesus' name, amen.

Day 16: Leading Your Family

Scripture:

"But as for me and my house, we will serve the Lord." — Joshua 24:15

Reflection

God designed men to lead — not as dictators, but as servant leaders who guide their homes with love, integrity, and spiritual strength.

Joshua stood before the nation of Israel and made a bold declaration: "As for me and my house, we will serve the Lord." He didn't wait for someone else to take responsibility. He led by example.

Every man who follows Jesus carries the same mantle. Whether you're a husband, father, or future leader of a family, your presence sets the spiritual tone of your home. You don't need to have all the answers — you just need to stay close to the One who does.

Leading your family means praying even when no one else feels like it, forgiving when it's hard, and loving with patience when life is stressful. It's showing your children that strength and gentleness can live in the same heart. It's being the first to say "I'm sorry" and the last to give up.

Your leadership isn't proven by control; it's proven by character and consistency. When your family sees you seeking God daily — reading His Word, worshiping, serving — they'll learn what faith looks like in motion.

And here's the truth: You don't have to be perfect to lead. You just have to be present. God will fill in the gaps when your heart is surrendered to Him.

Action Step

Take a moment to pray over your household today.

If you're married, pray with your spouse.

If you're a father, speak a blessing over your children.

If you're single, pray over the family you come from and the one God may still build through you.

Declare aloud: "As for me and my house, we will serve the Lord."

Prayer

Father, thank You for trusting me with the power and authority as I answer the call to lead. Teach me to lead with humility, courage, and compassion. Let my home be filled with Your presence and peace. As for me and my house, we will serve You and your Kingdom — today and always.

In Jesus' name, amen.

Day 17: Honoring Women

Scripture:

"Husbands, love your wives, just as Christ loved the church and gave himself up for her." — Ephesians 5:25

Reflection

Honor is the language of the Kingdom.

And one of the clearest ways a man shows his walk with God is by how he honors the women in his life — his wife, mother, sisters, daughters, and even strangers.

In a world that often objectifies women or diminishes their worth, godly men are called to be different. To honor a woman means to see her as God sees her — created in His image, deserving of dignity, protection, and love.

Jesus modeled this perfectly. He spoke to women others ignored. He defended them when society shamed them. He elevated their worth when others dismissed it. That's what Kingdom love looks like — not control, but covering; not dominance, but devotion.

For husbands, leading in love means serving like Christ — sacrificially, patiently, and selflessly. For single men, honoring women means guarding your eyes, your heart, and your intentions. It's treating every woman as someone's daughter — and ultimately, God's.

True strength isn't in how loudly you speak, but in how gently you lead. Honor builds trust. It restores hearts. It shows the world what divine love looks like in human form.

When Kingdom Men of God rise to honor women, families heal, generations shift, and the Kingdom Of Heaven advances.

Action Step

Show honor today in a tangible way.

If you're married, express gratitude to your wife — not just with words, but through action.

If you're single, find a way to encourage or support a woman in your life with pure motives and respect.

Ask God to help you reflect His heart toward every woman you encounter.

Prayer

Lord, thank You for the women You've placed in my life. Teach me to love, serve, and honor them as You do. Let my words and actions reflect Your respect and compassion. Make me a Kingdom Man who brings healing and honor wherever I go. In Jesus' name, amen.

Day 18: Forgiving Like Christ

Scripture:

"Bear with each other and forgive one another if any of you has a grievance against someone. Forgive as the Lord forgave you." — Colossians 3:13

Reflection

Forgiveness is one of the hardest things a man can do — and one of the most powerful.

(Matthew 6:14)

This is one of the most powerful lessons The Kingdom Man learns

It's not a feeling; it's a choice. A decision to release the debt, even when the wound still aches.
Jesus set the standard for forgiveness not from a place of comfort, but from the cross. As He hung in agony, He prayed, "Father, forgive them." That wasn't weakness — it was divine strength. The world teaches revenge; the Kingdom teaches release.

Unforgiveness is like carrying a heavy chain — it binds your spirit, drains your peace, and clouds your joy. When you forgive, you don't excuse what was done; you simply refuse to let it rule over you anymore. You hand it over to the only Judge who sees all things clearly.

This is a key to fruit that remains

Sometimes the hardest person to forgive is yourself. But the same grace that covers others covers you too. Christ's blood doesn't halfway cleanse — it washes completely.

Forgiving like Christ means choosing love when it hurts, mercy when it's undeserved, and peace when bitterness calls your name.

It's not easy, but it's freeing — and freedom is discovered where forgiveness begins. The Kingdom Man knows evil will never overcome evil.

Action Step

Think of someone — or even yourself — you've been holding resentment toward.

Write their name down and pray: "Lord, I release them into Your hands."

You don't need to feel it to mean it. Obedience opens the door for healing.

If possible, take a step toward reconciliation or simply let go in prayer.

Prayer
Father, thank You for the gift of forgiving. Help me to extend that same grace to others that I may bear eternal fruit in Heavenly places. Holy Spirit I ask you to reveal any hidden places and hurts or resentments. Give me strength and wisdom in this area of my Kingdom Man walk.

Heal my heart, free me from bitterness, and let Your love flow through me.

In Jesus' name, amen.

Day 19: Serving Others Scripture:

"For even the Son of Man did not come to be served, but to serve, and to give his life as a ransom for many." — Mark 10:45

Reflection

The truest sign of greatness in God's Kingdom isn't how many people follow you — it's how many people you serve.

Jesus — the Son of God, Creator of all things — wrapped a towel around His waist and washed the feet of His disciples. In that moment, He turned the world's definition of leadership upside down. He showed that authority is proven through humility, not control.

Service is love in motion. It's choosing to put others before yourself. It's doing the small, unseen things with a willing heart — not for recognition, but because you carry the heart of your Savior.

The world says, "Look out for yourself." Jesus says, "Lay yourself down." The greatest men in the Kingdom are those who serve quietly, give generously, and love sacrificially.

When you serve others, you reflect the character of Christ — the One who came not to be served, but to give His life for others. Every act of service, no matter how small, echoes in eternity.

If you want to lead like Jesus, start by serving like Him.

Action Step

Find one practical way to serve today — at home, work, church, or in your community.

Help someone without expecting anything in return.

Ask the Holy Spirit to make your heart sensitive to the needs around you, and act immediately when you feel that gentle nudge to help.

Prayer

Lord, make me a servant like You.

Help me to see the needs of others and respond with compassion. Let my hands, words, and actions reveal Your love to the world. In Jesus' name, amen.

Day 20: The Power of Brotherhood

Scripture:

"Two are better than one, because they have a good return for their labor: If either of them falls down, one can help the other up." — Ecclesiastes 4:9–10

Reflection

Lone wolves don't last long in the Kingdom.

Every man needs brothers who will pray for him, challenge him, and pick him up when life knocks him down.

Brotherhood is not a casual friendship — it's a covenant connection. It's knowing that you have men who will stand beside you when the battle gets heavy. It's being surrounded by those who see both your calling and your flaws, yet choose to walk with you anyway.

The Bible is filled with examples of powerful brotherhoods:

Moses had Aaron, David had Jonathan, Paul had Timothy, and Jesus had the Twelve. None of them fulfilled their calling alone. Each of them drew strength, accountability, and courage from godly partnership.

Real brotherhood sharpens your soul. It's built on honesty, not image — on truth, not talk. It means having men who will tell you when you're drifting, pray with you when you're weary, and celebrate when you overcome.

The enemy knows the power of unity. That's why he tries to isolate men with pride, shame, or busyness. But when brothers link arms in prayer and purpose, hell takes notice. A united band of men walking in truth and love is unstoppable.

You weren't meant to do life alone. Find your brothers — and fight for them.

Action Step

Reach out to one or two men of faith and strengthen that connection.

Plan a time to pray together, share honestly about life, or simply encourage one another.

If you've been distant, take the first step — send the text, make the call, start the conversation. Brotherhood grows when it's intentional.

Prayer

Father, thank You for the gift of brotherhood.
Surround me with godly men who strengthen my faith and hold me accountable.

Help me to be that kind of brother — loyal, prayerful, and strong in love.

In Jesus' name, amen.

Week 4: Purpose & Legacy — where faith becomes action, and a kingdom man's walk starts shaping the world around him.

Day 21: Love in Action

Scripture:"Dear children, let us not love with words or speech but with actions and in truth." — 1 John 3:18

Reflection

Love is not just something you feel — it's something you do and a person to become.

Real love is seen in how you treat people, how you serve when it's inconvenient, and how you forgive when it's undeserved.

The world talks a lot about love but often confuses it with emotion or attraction. The Kingdom Man love is deeper — it's sacrificial, steady, and strong. It's not powered by feelings but by faith. Jesus didn't just talk about love; He demonstrated it. He touched the untouchable, forgave the guilty, and gave His life for those who mocked Him.

For The Kingdom Man of God, love isn't weakness — it's warfare. It pushes back darkness, disarms pride, and heals what hatred has broken. When you love others through your actions, you're revealing the very heart of God.

Every act of kindness — every time you choose compassion

over anger, mercy over revenge, or generosity over greed — you are advancing God's Kingdom. Love in action changes hearts, including your own.

This kind of love takes courage. It means loving people who can't repay you, blessing those who hurt you, and showing grace even when it's not convenient. But when you do, you carry the fragrance of Christ into every space you walk into.

Action Step

Receive the love of God through thanksgiving and gratitude.

Put your love into action today.

Find a way to tangibly show God's love –- buy someone a meal, encourage a stranger, call someone you've avoided, or forgive someone who wronged you.

Pray before you act and ask God to guide you to someone who needs His love today.

Prayer

Father, help me love not just in words but in deeds.

Perfect love casts out all fear. Take away any fears or doubts in my heart.

Fill my heart with compassion that moves me to action.

Let my life be a reflection of Your love, reaching those who need it most.

In Jesus' name, amen.

Day 22: Faith That Moves Mountains

Scripture:

"Truly I tell you, if you have faith as small as a mustard seed, you can say to this mountain, 'Move from here to there,' and it will move. Nothing will be impossible for you." — Matthew 17:20

Reflection

Faith isn't about how big the problem looks — it's about how deeply it's rooted in belief powered by the love of God.

Jesus said that even faith as small as a mustard seed can move mountains. He wasn't exaggerating; He was revealing a Kingdom principle: God doesn't need your perfection — He needs your heart of belief.

We all face mountains — obstacles that seem unmovable: fear, addiction, doubt, broken relationships, or financial struggle. But mountains don't move because you shout louder; they move because you trust deeper.

Real faith starts small but grows through obedience. Every time you choose to believe God's Word over what you see, your faith strengthens. Every time you pray instead of panic, obey instead of hesitate, you're exercising spiritual muscle.

Mountain-moving faith doesn't come from having all the answers. It comes from knowing the One who does. It's quiet confidence in a God who has never failed His people — and won't start with you.

Faith doesn't deny the mountain; it declares that God is greater than the mountain. And when you keep walking in trust, even the things that looked impossible will begin to shift.

You were not called to live a life of small belief — you were called to live a life that believes a big God for big things.
(Colossians 1:16-20)

Action Step

Identify one "mountain" in your life — something that's felt impossible.
Write it down, and every day this week, speak to it in faith:
"God, I believe You are greater than this mountain. I trust You to move it in Your time."

> Refuse to let fear have the final word. Keep standing on the promise.

Prayer

Lord, strengthen me in my faith today.

Release the gift of faith upon my life.

Release to me the ears to hear faith.

Release the substance and the unction.

Help my unbelief when I can't see the way forward.

I trust You to move mountains, open doors, and do what only You can do.

Let my faith be pleasing and bring You glory.

In Jesus' name, amen.

Day 23: Building on the Rock

Scripture:

"Therefore everyone who hears these words of mine and puts them into practice is like a wise man who built his house on the rock." — Matthew 7:24

Reflection

Every man is building something — a career, a family, a reputation, a legacy.

But the real question is: What are you building on?

Jesus told a simple yet profound story of two builders. Both faced the same storm, but only one house stood firm — the one built on the rock. The difference wasn't in their tools or talent, but in their foundation.

The "rock" isn't just hearing God's Word — it's doing it. It's applying truth when it costs you, obeying when it's uncomfortable, and trusting when it's unclear. *(James 1:22)*

Storms will come — not if, but when. The winds of temptation, loss, and disappointment will test every structure of your life. But when your foundation is Christ, you don't crumble; you endure.

Building on the Rock takes time and discipline. It's daily prayer, consistent obedience, and steady surrender. It's choosing character over convenience.

And the reward? Stability. Peace. Strength. You may bend, but you won't break — because your roots are deep in the unshakable Word of God.

A man who builds on the Rock doesn't just survive

storms; he becomes a shelter for others during them.

He becomes The Kingdom Man.

Action Step

Take time today to evaluate your foundation.

Ask yourself: Am I building on God's truth or my own understanding?

Identify one area of life where you've been relying on your own strength, and intentionally bring it back under Christ's authority.

Prayer

Lord, help me build my life on You —- the solid Rock that never shifts. Teach me to obey Your Word and trust You through every storm. Let my life stand as a testimony of Your strength and faithfulness. In Jesus' name, amen.

Day 24: Perseverance Through Pain

Scripture:

"We also glory in our sufferings, because we know that suffering produces perseverance; perseverance, character; and character, hope." — Romans 5:3–4

Reflection

Pain has a way of revealing what's real.

Anyone can praise God when life is easy, but true faith is proven in the fire — when everything in you wants to quit, yet you choose to stand anyway.

Paul understood that suffering isn't wasted. Every trial, every setback, every heartbreak becomes a tool in God's hand to shape your spirit. Pain doesn't just test your faith; it builds it. Through endurance, you develop strength that can't be faked — character that shines when everything else is shaking.

Perseverance isn't about pretending everything's fine; it's about refusing to give up when it's not. It's trusting that even when life hurts, God is still good.

When you keep pressing forward through pain, you declare to the world that your faith isn't fragile — it's anchored in something eternal.

Jesus modeled this perfectly. He endured the cross, despising its shame, because of the joy set before Him — your redemption. That same perseverance lives in you through the Holy Spirit.

So don't curse the pain. Let it press you deeper into purpose. What feels like breaking might actually be God's way of building something unshakable inside you.

Action Step

Think of a painful season you're walking through or have walked through recently.

Ask God, "What are You trying to teach me through this?"

Write down one thing you've learned or one way you've grown because of that trial — then thank Him for using even your pain for good.

Prayer

Father, thank You for turning pain into purpose.

Give me strength to persevere when life gets heavy and grace to trust You through every season.

Let my trials shape me, not break me, and let my endurance bring You glory.

In Jesus' name, amen.

Notes_____

Day 25: Vision from God

Scripture:

"Write the vision and make it plain on tablets, that he may run who reads it." — Habakkuk 2:2

Reflection

Every great move of God begins with a vision.

Vision is more than a dream — it's a divine revelation of what could be when you walk in obedience to what God has shown you.

Habakkuk was told to "write the vision and make it plain," not because God needed a reminder, but because we do. When you write it down, you anchor your purpose. You create a record of what God spoke so that when doubt tries to whisper, you can look back and remember His promise.

But vision without discipline becomes fantasy. It's one thing to see; it's another to run with what you've seen. True vision demands prayer, patience, and persistence. It may not happen overnight — but if God gave it, He will bring it to pass in His timing.

A man with no vision drifts; a man with God's vision builds.

Vision gives direction to your energy, meaning to your pain, and endurance for your journey. It's the compass that keeps you moving forward when life tries to pull you backward.

And here's the truth: the vision God gives you isn't just for you — it's meant to bless others. When you walk in it, your obedience becomes the doorway to someone else's breakthrough.

Action Step

Set aside quiet time today to ask God for fresh vision.

Write down what He places in your heart — it could be for your family, ministry, business, or personal growth.

Pray over it daily, and begin taking one small, consistent step toward it.

Prayer

Father, thank You for giving me vision and purpose.

Help me to see with eyes of faith, to hear Your direction clearly, and to move with courage and boldness.
Let the vision You've placed in me glorify You and impact others for Your Kingdom.

In Jesus' name, amen.

Day 26: Generosity and Grace

Scripture:

"A generous man will prosper; he who refreshes others will himself be refreshed." — Proverbs 11:25

Reflection

Generosity is the overflow of a grateful heart.

It's not about how much you have — it's about how much you're willing to release.

In the Kingdom, generosity and grace walk hand in hand. God has poured His grace freely into your life — forgiveness, peace, provision, and purpose. The more you recognize how much you've received, the more freely you'll give.

The world says to hold tightly, protect your resources, and look out for yourself first. But God's economy runs on a different principle: the more you give, the more room you make to receive.

Generosity isn't just about money; it's about your time, your encouragement, your compassion, and your willingness to bless others without expecting anything in return.

Jesus lived generously. He gave His attention to the overlooked, His mercy to the broken, His strength to the weary — and His life for all of us. When you walk in that same spirit, you become a reflection of His heart on earth.

And here's the secret: generosity doesn't drain you — it refreshes you. When you pour into others, God fills you back up in ways you can't
imagine. *Grace flows through open hands.*

Action Step

Do one generous act today — give without expecting to receive.

It could be financial, but it might also be time, encouragement, or prayer.

Ask God to make you sensitive to a need around you, and be quick to respond with joy, not hesitation.

Prayer

Lord, thank You for Your endless grace and generosity toward me. Help me to give freely, love deeply, and live with open hands.

Make me a vessel of blessing, and let my life reflect Your generous heart.

In Jesus' name, amen.

Day 27: Men Who Carry The Fire

Scripture:

"For our God is a consuming fire." – Hebrews 12:29

Reflection

A true Kingdom Man doesn't just talk about the fire of God–he carries it. The presence of the Holy Spirit burns within him, refining his character, consuming his pride and igniting passion for righteousness.

The fire is not emotional hype; it's a holy power that transforms you from the inside out. The Kingdom Man who carries the fire becomes a living altar–his life burns continually before the Lord.

God is calling men in this generation to walk as burning ones. Men whose hearts are purified, whose motives are holy, and whose actions release the fragrance of His presence and the power of his Kingdom. When you carry the fire, compromise can't stay. Sin loses its grip. Fear has no place. You become a vessel through which God displays His power and glory on earth.

Ask yourself today– is the fire still burning, or has it been dimmed by distraction, weariness, or compromise?

Stir it again. Fan the flame. Let the world see Christ in you, the hope of glory.

Action Step

Is there anything in your life that's trying to extinguish your fire?

How can you keep you heart burning for God daily to seek the

Kingdom?

Who in your life needs to encounter the fire of the Holy Spirit through you?

Prayer

Father, let your holy fire burn within me. Consume everything that is not of You.

Ignite fresh passion for Your presence and Your purpose in my heart.

Make me a Kingdom Man who carries Your fire everywhere I go— a man of purity, power, and perseverance. In Jesus name, amen

Day 28: Finishing Strong

Scripture:

"I have fought the good fight, I have finished the race, I have kept the faith." — 2 Timothy 4:7

Reflection

It's not how you start that defines you — it's how you finish.

It's not about how you were born or where you were born, it's about why you were born.

The world celebrates fast starts and instant results, but the Kingdom honors those who endure. Paul's life wasn't easy — he was beaten, imprisoned, betrayed, and misunderstood — yet when his time came, he could boldly declare, "I have finished the race."

Finishing strong requires more than enthusiasm; it requires commitment and endurance.

It means staying faithful when excitement fades, holding onto vision when the road grows rough, and trusting God when outcomes don't match expectations.

Every man who walks with Jesus will face moments when quitting seems easier. But remember: the same grace that saved you will sustain you. God never asked you to finish the race in your own strength — He promised to carry you through if you keep your eyes on Him.

A strong finish isn't about perfection — it's about persistence. It's showing up one more day, praying one more prayer, forgiving one more time, and believing one more promise.

It's standing before the Father someday and hearing, "Well done, good and faithful servant."

Don't let weariness steal your focus. The finish line is closer than you think — and the reward waiting for you is worth every step.

Action Step

Look back over your journey with God.

Where have you been tempted to give up — on a calling, relationship, or dream?

Ask the Holy Spirit for renewed strength and determination to finish what God started in you.

Write down Philippians 1:6 ("He who began a good work in you will carry it on to completion") and declare it daily.

Prayer

Father, give me the strength to finish well.

When I grow tired, remind me that Your grace is enough.

Help me stay faithful until the very end, and let my life bring glory to Your name.

In Jesus' name, amen.

Day 29: Legacy of Faith

Scripture:

"The righteous man walks in his integrity; his children are blessed after him." — Proverbs 20:7

Reflection

Every man leaves a legacy. The question isn't if you'll leave one — it's what kind.

Legacy isn't built in a moment; it's shaped over a lifetime of small, faithful choices.

A true legacy isn't about wealth, titles, or recognition — it's about impact. It's the spiritual footprint you leave behind in the lives you've touched. It's the prayers you prayed that still echo in your family, the truth you spoke that still guides others, and the faith you lived that still inspires long after you're gone.

The Bible says the righteous man walks in integrity, and his children are blessed after him. That means your faith today becomes someone else's foundation tomorrow. Every time you choose obedience, you're building something eternal.

Abraham's faith blessed generations he never saw. David's worship shaped a nation long after his death. Your story can do the same. You don't have to be famous to be influential — you just have to be faithful. His blessing upon your life is for 1000 generations.

When you walk in righteousness, you're planting seeds that your children, grandchildren, and spiritual sons will one day harvest. The world may forget your name, but Heaven will remember your obedience.

So keep living with eternity in mind. Let your life tell a story of faith, courage, and love that points every generation back to Jesus.

Action Step

Take time to reflect on the kind of legacy you're building.

Write down three words you want people to say about your life when you're gone — then live intentionally toward those words today.

Pray for your family and future generations, that they will continue the faith you've begun.

Prayer

Father, thank You for the legacy of faith You're building in my life.

Help me to walk with integrity, love with consistency, and lead with humility.

Let my life plant seeds that will bear fruit for generations to come. In Jesus' name, amen.

Day 30: The Crown Awaits

Scripture:

"Now there is in store for me the crown of righteousness, which the Lord, the righteous Judge, will award to me on that day—and not only to me, but also to all who have longed for his appearing." — 2 Timothy 4:8

Reflection

Every race has a finish line. Every battle ends in victory for those who endure to the end.

The Apostle Paul, nearing the close of his life, looked beyond the pain of his present and fixed his eyes on eternity. He saw not loss, but reward — "a crown of righteousness."

This is the destiny of every Kingdom Man who walks faithfully with Jesus. The world's trophies fade, but Heaven's rewards endure forever. The crown Paul spoke of isn't made of gold or jewels — it's the reward of a life lived in obedience, perseverance, and love for Christ.

Throughout this journey, you've learned what it means to live as a Kingdom man — strong in faith, humble in heart, bold in purpose, and steady under pressure. But the journey doesn't end here. This 30- day devotional isn't a finish line; it's a launching point.

The same God who called you to rise will empower you to keep rising — through every challenge, every season, and every assignment. And one day, when your race is complete, you'll stand before Him — not in shame, but in victory — and hear the words that every faithful servant longs to hear:

"Well done."

Until that day, keep running your race. Keep fighting the good fight. Keep loving Jesus with all your heart. The crown awaits — and so does the King.

Action Step

Take time today to reflect on your 30-day journey.

Write down the biggest truth or transformation God has stirred in your heart.

Then, dedicate your next season to living it out with boldness and consistency.

Pray for endurance to keep pressing forward until the day you see Jesus face to face.

Prayer

Lord, thank You for walking with me through this 30-day journey. Strengthen me to keep running my race with endurance and joy.

Let my life bring glory to You until the day I receive the crown that never fades.

I live for Your honor, Your Kingdom, and Your name

I live to be a Kingdom Man

In Jesus' name, amen.

7-Day Reflection — Men After God's Heart

Theme: A Week of Fire, Focus, and Faith

After seven days of pressing into the Word, pause to let the Spirit of God speak deeply.

This week has not been about information — it's been about transformation.

Every devotional, every prayer, and every moment of reflection was designed to rekindle your faith, renew your focus, and refine your purpose as a Kingdom man.

---

1. Rekindled Fire

Has your passion for the presence of God grown?

Where has the flame dimmed?

The fire of revival begins in the secret place — reignite it there.

2. Restored Focus

Are your eyes still fixed on Jesus, or have distractions pulled your attention away?

True leadership begins with clear spiritual vision.

3. Renewed Faith

Faith isn't proven in moments of ease but in the heat of challenge.

Ask God to stretch your faith beyond comfort into confidence in His power.

4. Refined Character

The Spirit is shaping you into the image of Christ.

What attitudes, habits, or fears has He exposed this week?

Surrender them to His refining fire.

5. Reclaimed Purpose

You were created to build, lead, and serve.

Your purpose is not just to survive — it's to advance the Kingdom.

Write down what God is calling you to step into next.

6. Renewed Authority

Walk boldly in the authority Jesus has given you.

You are not powerless; you are anointed to bring transformation.

Declare that authority over your home, your work, and your city.

7. Released Power

The same Spirit that raised Christ from the dead lives in you.

Let that truth move from theology to reality.

You are a carrier of the power of God — release it in love, service, and faith.

Prayer of Renewal

Father, I thank You for all You have done in these seven days.
Rekindle the fire within me, restore my faith, and renew my focus.
Let my life be a reflection of Your power and presence.
I choose to walk as a Kingdom man — full of faith, fire, and purpose.
In Jesus' mighty name, amen.

Made in the USA
Middletown, DE
16 November 2025